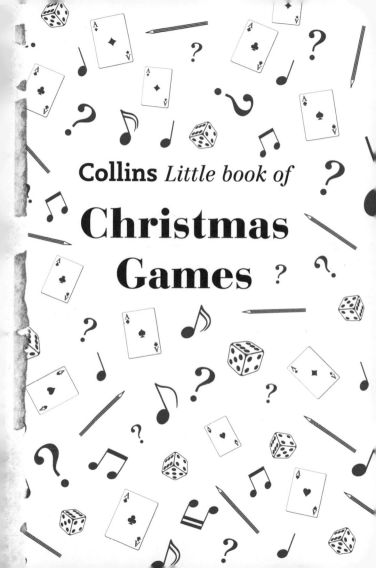

Collins *Little book of*

Christmas
Games

HarperCollins Publishers
Westerhill Road
Bishopbriggs
Glasgow
G64 2QT

First Edition 2012

Reprint 10 9 8 7 6 5 4 3 2 1 0

© HarperCollins Publishers 2012

ISBN 978-0-00-748301-3

Collins® is a registered trademark of
HarperCollins Publishers Limited

www.collinslanguage.com

A catalogue record for this book is
available from the British Library

Typeset by Davidson Publishing
Solutions, Glasgow

Printed and bound at Leo Paper
Products Ltd

Acknowledgements
We would like to thank those authors
and publishers who kindly gave
permission for copyright material
to be used in the Collins Corpus.
We would also like to thank Times
Newspapers Ltd for providing
valuable data.

Author
Mike Munro

Editors
Gerry Breslin
Freddy Chick

Illustrations
Pat Murray

Design
Catherine Lutman

For the Publisher
Lucy Cooper
Julianna Dunn
Kerry Ferguson
Elaine Higgleton
Susanne Reichert

CONTENTS

Introduction – why play games at Christmas?

Christmas is a time when people get together, and given the kind of weather likely to prevail in the Northern hemisphere, they're mostly going to get together indoors. There'll be plenty of eating and drinking, of course, Christmas being the one big annual blowout that everyone feels entitled to indulge in. But if you've got a house full of people, how are you going to entertain them after the festive meal is over and the dishes are cleared away?

You could always put the telly on but people can watch the box any old time, and presumably they didn't leave the comfort of their own homes just to slump in front of the screen at your house. Christmas should be special! It should be fun!

Games are about being active and getting everyone involved. Your guests may all be family members who know each other well, but maybe the older and younger generations aren't all that used to spending time together. Games will soon have everyone competing or co-operating. You may have more of a mix of people, perhaps with friends and neighbours who don't know one another. Games will break the ice! Many people complain that nowadays kids spend too much time staring at computer screens or gluing their noses to the latest hand-held electronic toy, exercising nothing but their thumbs, in the relentless pursuit of beeps and explosions. Get them playing physical games like Musical Chairs and you'll be giving them an outlet for their boundless energy as well as physical exercise. Young minds will gain from the mental workout offered by word or number games too. Being painlessly required to think, they might even learn a thing or two without it being a chore!

So get everyone in the same room, one which is warm and comfortable. Make sure they all have somewhere to sit, or, if physical games are on the agenda, clear enough floor space to allow plenty of room for exuberance. Have plenty of drinks and snacks on hand to keep the players from flagging. Now let the games begin!

Card Games

Gin Rummy

What is it?
Something to do with strong drink? Alas no, despite the boozy name! This is a game, for two players, in which you have to put together sets and sequences of cards.

Here's what you need
An ordinary pack of cards, a pen and some paper for keeping track of the scores.

How to play
The dealer deals each player ten cards, leaving the rest of the pack in the middle of the table, then turns the top card of this pile face up, putting it beside the main pile. Meanwhile the players are looking at the cards they've been dealt and sorting them into sets. What makes a set? Any three or four cards that have the same value (like three eights) or belong to a sequence in the same suit (like the eight, nine, ten and jack of hearts).

If it's your turn to play first, look at the card that is lying face up. If you can use it to help make up a set, pick it up. If you don't want it, take the first card from the top of the pile. You don't have to keep this card if it's of no use, but if

you do you have to get rid of one of yours and add it to the face-up pile. Every player should always have ten cards in their hand.

How to win

The cards you're holding may change as the game goes on and you spot possibilities of better sets, but keep a close eye on your hand. As soon as you realise that any unmatched cards you have will add up to ten or less, when it's your turn to play you lay your cards down, and then you've won that round!

If you're very very lucky, you might find that the cards you are dealt to begin with can be sorted immediately into a winning hand (spot the players feverishly assessing their cards right after the deal!) but this doesn't happen very often.

What's the score?

Face cards are worth 10 points; aces 1 point, and all other cards at their face value. If all of your cards are in sets when you lay them down, this is called a Gin Hand, and you win 25 points, plus the values of the other player's unmatched cards.

Losing players can reduce the number of points that the winner gains from them by adding, whenever possible, their unmatched cards to the winner's sequences.

Pontoon/21

What is it?

This is a simple game, as long as you can count up to 21! In America they call it Blackjack, and it's often used for gambling, but you can play it just for fun!

Here's what you need

An ordinary pack of cards and the ability to add up to 21.

How to play

The idea is to have cards that add up to 21, or as close to that as you can get without going over. To begin, the dealer deals each player one card, turning the card they deal themselves face up. Then the dealer deals one more card each, but does not turn up his or her own second card.

Each player adds up their cards. (Aces count as one or eleven.) If they immediately total 21 (for example, an ace and a face card or a ten) then this is a potentially winning hand and the player must say 'Pontoon' and lay their cards down face up.

If not you're faced with a choice of two options: Stick or Twist? You can ask for another card by saying 'Twist' and

then see how close you are to 21. You might risk another twist to edge even closer to the magic number, but beware! If your new card takes your total over 21 then you are 'bust', and you lose.

If your cards total a number close to 21 (like 19 or 20) you can play it safe and show that you're happy with what you've got by saying 'Stick'.

Winning

When all players are sticking or bust, the dealer turns up his or her second card. If this results in 21, the dealer immediately beats everyone except those with 21 too. The dealer can 'twist' more cards, or can stick when he or she reckons another card will 'bust' the hand.

Beggar-my-neighbour

What is it?

This game is all about taking all your opponent's cards away. That's why it's also known as Strip Jack Naked. (Note: no clothes need to be removed during this game nor do you have to play with your actual neighbours. There are games, not included here, which involve both!)

Here's what you need

An ordinary pack of cards.

How to play

Each player takes half of the pack of cards, placing their pile face down. The first to play takes a card from the top of his or her lot and lays it face up, then the other player does the same, laying their card on top of the first. Depending on how the cards run, this can lead to quite a large pile accumulating in the middle. They keep repeating this action until one of them turns up an ace or a face card.

If you turn up one of these cards your opponent has to give you some of his or her cards: one for a jack, two for a queen, three for a king, and four for an ace. After that,

the player who played the ace or face card gets to take all of the cards that have piled up so far and put them at the bottom of their pile. They then restart play by turning up another card.

But, and here's the crux of the matter, if one of the cards that the penalized player has to hand over is an ace or face card then the payment is reversed and the first player has to hand over the appropriate number of cards. This see-sawing between the players can go on for ages!

How to win

You keep playing until one of you has all of the cards in your pile. That's how you beggar your neighbour!

Old Maid

What is it?

This is all about getting rid of cards. Don't be left holding the one that can't be matched!

Here's what you need

An ordinary pack of cards, with one card removed.

How to play

Start by taking one card out of the pack, usually something memorable like the queen of clubs. This means that there's only one black queen left, the queen of spades, which can't be paired with another card.

Deal out all the cards among the players. Each player looks at their hand and takes out any pairs, placing them down face up. A pair needs to be two cards of the same value (such as threes, jacks, etc) and of the same colour (red or black). Remember it's only pairs that count. If you have three cards of the same value you can only take out two.

Once everyone has discarded their pairs, the dealer lays his or her hand face down to let the next player chose one of them. This player checks if a pair can be made with

this new card and, if so, lays it down before allowing the next player to take a card from his or her remaining cards. Keep playing until no-one has any cards left except one, the Old Maid!

Snap

What is it?

For a few golden months in every young life, 'Snap!' is the funniest thing on the planet. Brilliantly simple, it is a definite classic.

Here's what you need

An ordinary pack of cards, or perhaps two packs if lots of you want to play.

How to play

Deal out all the cards between the players so that each has a stack, all face down. The first to go takes one card from the top of their pile and, without looking at it, lays it down face up in the middle. The next player does the same and so on, until somebody lays down a card that has the same value (such as a four, king, etc of any suit) as the one before.

The person who reacts quickest and is the first to cry out 'Snap!' wins all the cards in the middle pile. This player then restarts play by laying down the next card, and so on. Look out for players getting over-excited as they become desperate to slap down a matching card!

Keep going until nobody has any cards left except the winner.

An optional penalty of giving your opponents one card if you wrongly cry 'Snap!' can be applied.

Go Fish

What is it?

In this game you have to collect sets of four cards of the same value. You will be amazed at how much pent up anger can be released by telling each other to 'go fish'!

Here's what you need

An ordinary pack of cards.

How to play

How many of you want to play? If there's two or three, you each get seven cards. If four, five or six, then each player is dealt five cards. The rest of the deck are laid face down in the middle.

After you've have had a chance to look at the cards in your hands, the first player to go can ask any other player if they have any specified cards. For example, if you have one or two threes you might ask 'George, do you have any threes?' But note, you can't ask for cards of a particular value if you don't have any of them to begin with.

If 'George' has any threes he has to give them to you, and you get another chance to ask for cards, either from 'George' or from any of the other players. You can keep

asking for cards until the person you ask doesn't have what you want. They will then say 'Go fish!' Then you have to take the card from the top of the pile in the middle and it's the next player's turn to ask.

As soon as you have four cards of the same value, you lay them down face up for all to see. If you're lucky enough to pick the last card of a set of four when you have been told to go fish, you can lay them down and it's still your turn. If you have no cards left you have to take one from the pile in the middle.

You keep playing until all possible sets of four have been laid down.

How to win

You win by collecting the most sets of four cards.

Sevens

What is it?

It's a case of getting rid of all of your cards!

Here's what you need

An ordinary pack of cards.

How to play

Deal out all of the cards amongst the people playing.

Have a look at your hand and arrange your cards according to suits. Whoever has the seven of hearts has to lay it face up in the middle. The player to the left can then place the seven of another suit beside the first seven, or place the six of hearts beneath the seven or the eight of hearts above it. If you don't have any of these cards the turn passes to the next player, but if you have a card you can play then you have to play it. In this way, players get rid of their cards by adding to these sequences.

How to win

Apart from being lucky in the cards you are dealt, you win by stopping other players from being able to play their cards. For example, if you have a seven of a

particular suit but not many other cards of that suit, try to avoid playing it. Similarly, if you can see that most of the low cards in a suit have been played, if you avoid playing a card of medium value then your opponents will be blocked from playing their high cards.

Cheat

What is it?

This is another game where you try to get rid of your cards, but kids especially love this because you're *encouraged* to cheat!

Here's what you need

An ordinary pack of cards.

How to play

Deal out all of the cards to the players. The first player lays down a number of cards (up to four) face down, saying what they are supposed to be, 'three sixes' for example. This is where cheating comes in! The cards might actually be three unmatchable ones that you want to dump. It's up to the other players whether they believe you or not.

Challenge

Anyone can challenge the person who has just laid down some cards by calling out 'Cheat!' and at this point the challenged player has to show what the cards actually were. If they have been caught cheating they are punished by having to pick up all of the discarded cards

so far and add them to their own total. But if they were telling the truth, the player who challenged has to pick up the pile.

Winning

The winner is the player who, by knowing when to cheat and when to challenge, succeeds in ending up with no cards left.

Paper & Pen Games

Hangman

What is it?

This is a guessing game, with players gathering clues, all in the effort to prevent a grisly execution!

Here's what you need

Pen and paper, along with the ability to spell!

How to play

One person thinks of a word, keeping it to themselves. They then make a series of dashes on the paper, one for each letter of the word in question. The other players take it in turns to suggest a letter that might appear in the mystery word.

If a letter is suggested that does not appear in the word, the puzzle-setter starts drawing the diagram of a man being hanged (a bit morbid, it's true, but this shows how old this game actually is!). The game goes on like this, with a part of the drawing being added for each wrong letter (one for each part of the gallows, one for an arm or a leg, and so on). Each wrong letter is also written beneath the drawing, just to remind you not to suggest it again.

When someone gets a letter right, it is written in above the relevant dash — in each place it occurs if it's used more than once in the word. Anyone who thinks they can guess what the word is without having to see all the letters in it can shout it out at any point, and if they're right the game is over. The first person to come up with the right answer wins the right to set the next mystery word. If nobody can work it out, the drawing is continued until the figure of the poor little man hanging from the gallows is completed.

How to vary it

If younger children are playing, the word to be guessed has to be fairly easy. But if older kids or adults are involved, more difficult words can be used, or even a short phrase like the title of a film of book. It's up to you!

Battleships

What is it?

Avast me hearties! All at sea for a game for two, based on naval battles of old, in which you have to sink your opponent's fleet before they sink yours.

Here's what you need

Pen and paper.

How to play

You start with grids drawn on paper, usually measuring ten squares by ten squares. You need two grids each, one for your own 'fleet' and one for the enemy fleet. Every square is identified by a number (1 to 10) and a letter (A to J). You can write in the letters on the horizontal leg and the numbers on the vertical leg, or the other way round, whatever you like.

What's a fleet made up of? Different people have different versions, but you'll probably want an aircraft carrier, a couple each of battleships, cruisers and destroyers, and maybe a submarine or two. You have to decide where on your home grid you want to place your ships and mark them in (preventing your opponent from

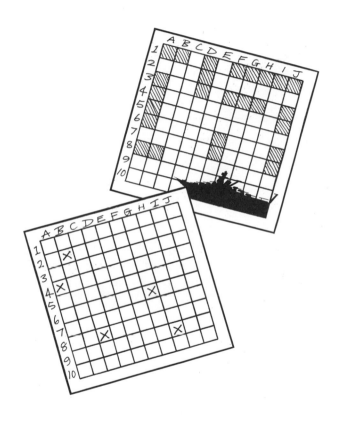

seeing this of course!). Bigger ships should take up more squares than smaller ones, so your aircraft carrier would occupy, say, four squares, your battleships three each, two for cruisers and destroyers, and one for a submarine. Put a letter (A for aircraft carrier, B for battleship, etc) in each square you pick until all of your fleet is in position.

Whoever has first go calls out the letter and number that identify a single square on the grid. This represents your fleet firing its guns at an enemy fleet which is out of sight. If this square on the other player's home grid is empty then it's their turn. But if the other player has a ship that occupies this square, he or she must say that this is a 'hit' and identify what kind of ship is involved.
The first player can then mark the relevant letter in this square on the enemy fleet grid. Put an X in any square that represents a 'miss', so that you don't make the mistake of choosing it again. Once all of the squares that make up a ship are hit, the ship is officially 'sunk' and is out of the game.

Play continues until one fleet is sunk.

How to win

Once you have scored a few hits you can begin to work out where the enemy's ships are positioned. Then you can start pinpointing individual squares to knock out ships completely rather than 'firing' at random.

Consequences

What is it?
This game involves working together to write stories but without anyone knowing what the others have written. The result will be an undoubtedly silly, occasionally naughty, and hopefully funny chain of events.

Here's what you need
Pen and paper.

How to play
You need at least two to play, but up to nine people could take part, if they have only one turn each.

Each player takes a piece of paper and writes an adjective on it, folds the paper so that what they've written can't be read, then passes it to the next player. Now it's their turn to write something and pass it on in the same way. The last person to write unfolds the sheet of paper and reads out the hilarious results!

You can decide for yourself what types of thing the successive players should write, but the most popular form of this game usually follows this sort of pattern:

1. an adjective for a man
2. a man's name
3. an adjective for a woman
4. a woman's name
5. where they met
6. what he said to her
7. what she said to him
8. what the consequence was
9. what the world said

For example ...

Here's one, just to show you how it might go. You're sure to be able to do much better when you give your imagination a free hand!

Muscular
Charlie
met *lovely*
Sarah
at *the museum.*
He said *'Would you like an ice cream?'.*
She said *'I don't like you'.*
The consequence was that *he joined the police force.*
The world said *'It's nice to be nice.'*

Doublets

What is it?

Lewis Carroll, the author of *Alice's Adventures in Wonderland*, loved to invent word games and this is one of his creations. The idea is to transform one word into another in as few moves as possible.

Here's what you need

Pen and paper. Good spelling and vocabulary skills are also useful!

How to play

You can play with two or more people taking turns, or you can give any number of people the same puzzle to solve on their own, with the winner being the one who takes the fewest steps.

Begin with two words that have the same number of letters. It's even more fun if they are linked in some way, maybe opposites. Write one at the top of a sheet of paper and one at the bottom. Now try to convert the first word into the second by changing one letter at a time. But each time you change a letter the result has to be a real word in its own right. No foreign words, nonsense or proper names!

Here's a couple of examples

Change HATE to LOVE:

HATE
HAVE
HIVE
LIVE
LOVE

Change SICK to WELL:

SICK
SILK
SILL
SELL
WELL

Bingo

What is it?

In this game players have to match numbers called at random to the numbers they have on their card. The winner is the first person to have all of their numbers matched.

Here's what you need

You've got to have bingo cards and counters. You can buy these ready-made if you're that organized, but it's easy to make your own. Each player will need a card with a selection of numbers marked on it, and no two cards can be the same.

Making the cards

Take a piece of fairly stiff card and mark a grid on it, measuring nine rows across and three rows down. Each horizontal row should contain five numbers, placed at random, leaving four blanks. Assign the numbers according to which column they go into:

> first column – numbers between one and ten
> second column – eleven to twenty
> third column – twenty-one to thirty

fourth column – thirty-one to forty
fifth column – forty-one to fifty
sixth column – fifty-one to sixty
seventh column – sixty-one to seventy
eighth column – seventy-one to eighty
ninth column – eighty-one to ninety.

Now write out the numbers 1 to 90 on another piece of card and cut them up so that every number is on a separate piece. These can be put into a hat or some other suitable container (not see-through!) to be drawn out later.

You will also need counters to place on your cards, covering the numbers that are called out. Tiddlywinks are good, and so are buttons, especially chocolate!

How to play

Nominate one person (the caller) to draw numbers out of the hat one at a time without looking at them and call them out. If you have any of the numbers on your card cover it with a counter. The first person to cover all of their numbers can shout 'Bingo!' They've won!

Beetle

What is it?

This is a game of chance – and drawing! – which revolves around the throw of a dice.

Here's what you need

Paper and pencils for everyone, and a dice.

How to play

The idea is to complete your own drawing of a beetle. You take turns throwing a dice and the number you throw decides which part of the beetle you get to add to your drawing. Here's a popular way of matching numbers to beetle parts (but you can always decide your own variation):

6. You have to throw a six to start, then you can draw the body.

5. Throw a five and draw the head.

4. A four lets you draw the tail.

3. Three gives you a leg (of which there are six, of course).

2.   Throw a two and draw a feeler (there should be two of these).

1.   A one is an eye (two of these).

How to win

The winner is the first player to complete their beetle drawing. Don't worry if you're no Leonardo da Vinci: it doesn't have to be a work of art to win!

Activity Games

Forfeits

What is it?

Forfeits is all about making people carry out a task which they probably would prefer not to do! Sometimes they are not used as a game but as a 'punishment' for the loser of another game, but you can play a game of forfeits for its own sake.

How to play

The first thing to do is decide how you are going to work out who does what. You could simply put names in a hat to be drawn out at random, but that's too dull! Why not have each player put something belonging to them onto a table or into a large container and let someone (the judge!) wearing a blindfold pick one out at a time? The judge then decrees what the owner of the item must do, without knowing who the person is.

What forfeits?

Everybody will have their own ideas for possible forfeits. The secret of success is to tailor them to the people taking part. Young kids will relish being told to do silly things while for older children and adults, things can get as risqué as you like or even involve consumption of alcoholic drinks. Here's some suggestions:

Kids

Tell a funny joke.

Do a silly dance.

Make an animal noise that everyone can recognize.

Adults

Kiss every other player of the opposite sex.

Answer three questions, replying only 'yes' or 'no'.

Down a nominated drink in one go.

Sing a nominated song.

The limits depend, of course, on your own imagination and what the players are prepared to put up with!

Blind Man's Buff

What is it?

One of the oldest games around, this is simply a 'catching' game in which the pursuer is handicapped by being blindfolded.

Here's what you need

A good-sized room or other empty space with anything that an unseeing person might stumble over moved out of the way. And a blindfold!

How to play

Once you've chosen the person who is going to do the chasing, they have to be blindfolded. They are then spun round two or three times to disorientate them before being released. They must then feel their way around, trying to catch any of the other players (who are free to dodge out of the way and to tease and taunt the blindfolded one by speaking, making noises, or even touching them briefly. Some players even take the chance of keeping perfectly still and silent to avoid being caught, but they have to make sure they're not breathing too heavily!)

Once the chaser manages to catch another player then that person has to take over the blindfold and the catching role. Play can continue in this way for as long as you like.

Change it around ...

If all the players know each other reasonably well, you can make it the rule that the chaser must not only catch another player but be able to say who they are.

Charades

What is it?

In this game one person has to act out, physically but silently, the name of a book, film, song, etc and the other players have to work out what it is from purely visual clues.

Here's what you need

There's no props or equipment needed – just some keen mimers and guessers!

How to play

Choose one person to play the first charade. The others guess the meanings of his or her mimes as each clue is offered. As soon as someone guesses correctly, the round is over and they get to play the next charade.

The basic mimes

You begin by identifying the genre of the mystery title.

Book mime opening a book.

Film The idea is to mime using an old-fashioned hand-cranked movie camera (a 1908/35m Parvo will do).

Song Mime the act of holding a microphone in front of your open mouth.

TV show Sketch a square in the air with your two pointing index fingers, mimicking a television screen.

Person Stand with your hands on your hips. Various conventions exist for specifying male or female; make sure everyone is agreed on which to use!

Once the genre is established, you can begin to put across the title itself. For this you need to start by establishing the number of words involved by holding up the appropriate amount of fingers.

Now you can mime individual words. You don't have to mime the first word first; go for the one that seems easiest to guess. Indicate its position in the title/name by holding up the appropriate number of fingers.

One approach is to break words down into syllables, acting them out individually. (For instance 'poke' for the start of 'Pocahontas'). You can show the number of syllables in your word by placing that number of fingers against your forearm, then repeat this gesture to show which syllable you're going to mime.

Another useful mime is the 'sounds like' gesture. If you tug your earlobe this is a signal that the word you're trying to put across sounds like another, easier-to-guess, word.

Encouraging the guessers

When somebody calls out the right answer to any of your clues, confirm this by pointing directly at them and nodding, or by touching a finger to the tip of your nose.

Squeak, Piggy, Squeak

What is it?

This is a bit like Blind Man's Buff, but if you're not 'it' you get to sit down!

Here's what you need

A blindfold and a number of chairs.

How to play

Arrange some chairs in a circle (one for each player except the one who's 'it').

Choose who's going first, then blindfold them and give them a cushion to hold. Everybody else then sits down, without saying a word. Spin the blindfolded person round two or three times then set them loose.

What they have to do is grope their way to one of the seated players, put the cushion in that person's lap, then sit on it. At this point they say the magic command 'Squeak, Piggy, Squeak!' and the sat-upon player has to make a piggy-like squeal. The blindfolded player then has to guess the other's identity purely from the noise they make, while the 'squeaker' tries to disguise the sound of their voice.

If the guess is correct, the two players change places and the seated person gets blindfolded. If the guess is off-target, the guesser is taken into the centre again so that play can restart. The seated players can meanwhile swap places if they like.

Hide and Seek

What is it?

Probably the simplest game of all. All you have to do is find people who are hiding from you.

Here's what you need

This is great fun to play outdoors, but in cold Christmas weather you need a house with plenty of good places to hide. Try to be ingenious!

How to play

Everyone assembles in one place to decide who's going to be 'it'. This person then covers their eyes (or closes them and turns to face the wall) and begins to count up to a specified number (usually a hundred). The others then scatter and go looking for likely hiding places while the count continues. When the counting finishes, the person who's 'it' calls out 'Ready or not, here I come!' and rushes off to find the others.

Anyone who is 'found' has to go back to the starting place and wait there while the searching continues. Play goes on until the searcher has ferreted everybody out or decides to give up when someone can't be found.

If everyone is found, the next person to be the seeker will be the one who was found first, otherwise the game must restart with the original seeker having another go.

Wink Murder

What is it?
Your chance to be a homicide detective!

Here's what you need
Enough slips of paper to have one for each player.

How to play
Mark an X on one of the paper slips, leaving all others blank, then put them into a hat or other non-see-through container and mix them up. Everyone draws out a slip. If yours has the X then you're the murderer – don't let anybody know!

The randomly selected psychopath has to 'kill' as many of the other players as possible without being detected. He or she does this by catching another player's eye and secretly winking at them. After waiting a few moments so that there's no obvious connection, the murdered player then stages a dramatic 'death'.

It's up to the other players to work out who the killer is. Anyone who thinks they know can accuse any other player. If they're wrong then they have to die too, but if they're right the round is over and play restarts from scratch.

Winning

Obviously even the most accomplished assassin can't get away with eliminating *all* of the other players. Once you're down to two, the innocent person has only to accuse the other, but a killer who can get this far is clearly a dangerous adversary!

Scissors, Paper, Stone

What is it?

The best way of deciding what Christmas telly to watch.

How to play

The players face each other holding one hand, clenched in a fist, upraised. They count 'one, two' each time lowering their hands, but on the count of three they must make one of three shapes with their hands.

These shapes are scissors (the first two fingers held apart like scissor-blades), paper (the hand open but with the fingers together) and stone (a clenched fist).

How to win

Winning depends on the hierarchy of these shapes. Scissors beats paper (because scissors will cut paper); stone beats scissors (because stone will blunt scissors); paper beats stone (because paper will wrap stone). If both players make the same shape, another round has to be played.

Because there is no sure way to win, with each shape able to be beaten by the right opposition, strategy comes into it. Try to work out what your opponent tends to do!

Hand Shadows

What is it?

This is simply the art of making shapes with your hands that create recognizable shadows.

Here's what you need

A fairly strong light source (even a powerful torch should do) and a white wall or blank screen to project shadows onto.

How to play

Someone who's good at this can quickly show the youngsters how to make the basic shapes, like the dog's head. More elaborate designs, often using both hands, will need a pattern to follow.

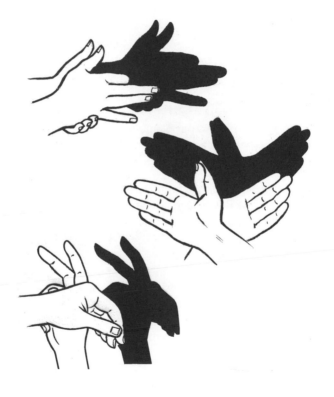

Sardines

What is it?

This is Hide and Seek with a twist! Everyone tries to hide in the same place!

Here's what you need

A house that not only has plenty of good places to hide, but has some that can squeeze in several people at once.

How to play

As in Hide and Seek, everybody assembles at the same starting point. But instead of one person closing their eyes and counting to a hundred, this time everybody does this, except the one who's 'it', who runs off and hides.

When the count is finished the pack of seekers must scatter and each on their own has to try and find the hider. You can't go round in twos and threes because (and here's the twist!) if you find the person who's hiding, you have to hide along with them. As more and more players stumble across the hiding place and jam themselves in, things can become pretty cramped. You end up looking like sardines in a tin, so hence the name!

Beware of giggling, though: too much will give the hiding place away too easily!

If everybody manages to hide, then the last player to find them becomes 'it' in the next round.

Oranges and Lemons

What is it?

Ideal for larger groups of young kids, this game involves both movement and singing, and its rather macabre conclusion has horrible appeal!

How to play

The kids line up in a column of pairs, then the first pair turn to face each other, grasping each other's hands in the air to form an arch. The other players then pass under this arch in pairs while everyone sings the traditional rhyme based on the churches of London:

> *'Oranges and lemons,'*
> *Say the bells of St Clement's.*

> *'You owe me five farthings,'*
> *Say the bells of St Martin's.*

> *'When will you pay me?'*
> *Say the bells of Old Bailey.*

> *'When I grow rich,'*
> *Say the bells of Shoreditch.*

> *'When will that be?'*
> *Say the bells of Stepney.*

'I do not know,'
Says the great bell of Bow.

Here comes a candle to light you to bed,
And here comes a chopper to chop off your head!

Here's where it gets serious

As the last line in sung, the kids making the arch
suddenly drop their linked arms, trapping the pair who
are currently passing underneath. These two are then
'out' and have to form another arch beside the first one.
The game restarts and carries on until there are more
arches than players and those still in the game have to
sprint to make it all the way through!

Hunt the Slipper

What is it?

A friendly introduction to the basics of shoplifting and an excellent game for kids and grown ups to play together.

How to play

Everyone sits on the floor in a circle. The one who's 'it' goes out of the room to let the others decide who's going to secretly hold the slipper. It doesn't have to be a slipper, of course. You can use a thimble or anything else as long as it's small enough to be hidden without too much trouble.

The other player now comes back in and has to guess who's got the slipper. This is where you have to be good at pretending – whether it's trying to look innocent if you've got the hidden item or throwing the seeker off the scent by looking guilty when you don't have it!

If you like you can advise the seeker when he or she is getting 'hot' (ie closer to the hidden object) or 'cold'.

When the slipper is found, the player holding it now becomes 'it' and play restarts.

What's the Time, Mr Wolf?

What is it?

A good party game for younger kids, best played somewhere there's room to run about.

How to play

Choose one of the kids to be Mr Wolf, who then stands facing a wall. Don't cry if you're picked; it's just as much fun to be Mr Wolf and be in control of the others as it is to be one of the potential 'victims'. The rest of the players line up several steps away, ideally as far as they can get in the space available. The game starts when they all say, together, 'What's the time, Mr Wolf?'

Mr Wolf decides what time he wants it to be and announces this, for example, 'It's four o'clock'. The players then take four steps towards him. It's two steps for two o'clock, and so on. Play continues in this way and excitement mounts as the distance between the players and Mr Wolf gets ever smaller.

When Mr Wolf decides play has gone on long enough, when he's next asked the time he cries out 'It's dinner time!' and he turns and tries to catch one of the players.

If he's successful, the caught player then takes his place as Mr Wolf.

Mousehole

What is it?

This game is based on place names, so you have to know your geography. Could be perfect for distracting that incredibly boring auntie or uncle who spends all Christmas talking about the route they took to arrive.

Here's what you need

Some sheets of paper and a pen, to keep track of the connections and let everyone see that the spelling is accurate.

How to play

Play begins with one player saying the name of a town in Britain. The next player then has to respond with the name of another British town which begins with the last letter of the first town. For example, if a player says 'Maidstone' the next player might say 'Edinburgh' and the next might come up with 'Hull'.

If a player's spelling lets them down and they make a false connection, they're out. The same applies if they can't think of anything (so if in the example above you say 'Halifax' instead of 'Hull' that'll leave the next player racking their brains or asking for a gazetteer!).

How to win

Whatever you do, try to avoid naming a town that ends with the letter M, because this allows another player to call out 'Mousehole!' which means they win the game.

Fizz Buzz

What is it?
This is a counting game that keeps you on your toes. Not recommended when you've had too many festive drinks!

How to play
Players take it in turns to say a number each in a count from one to a hundred. Where it gets tricky is that you have to substitute the word 'fizz' or 'buzz' for certain numbers that are decided in advance. A popular way to play is that 'fizz' has to take the place of the number three or any multiple of it, and 'buzz' has to replace five or any multiple of that.

Here's how that would go:

> 'one, two, fizz, four, buzz, fizz, seven, eight, fizz, buzz, eleven …' and so on.

If you get mixed up and make a mistake, especially if you forget to say fizz or buzz, you're out! Once everyone gets the hang of it, the speed of play can really take off until all but the coolest heads are in a spin!

In the Manner of …

What is it?

This is like charades, but with players having to act out a given adverb. It's a case of Show *not* Tell!

How to play

The first player thinks up an adverb, but does not tell the other players what it is. It's up to the others to work it out by asking him or her to perform an action in the manner of the adverb. This is where it becomes inventive, not to mention silly!

Let's say the adverb is 'cheerfully'. Another player might call out 'washing the car' and so the first player mimes doing exactly that, in a cheerful manner. Straightforward enough, you might say, but what if the action called for is 'breaking up with someone' or 'burying your pet goldfish'? Not so easy!

The guessers depend on the acting skills of the first player in solving the puzzle, but, on the other hand, setting ridiculous tasks is as much part of the fun as working out the answer!

Scavenger Hunt

What is it?
Players have to search for specified objects, the winner being the one who first locates them all.

Here's what you need
Depending on the space you have available, you can stage this over a whole house or restrict it to one room – especially if younger kids are playing. Lists of items to be located must be prepared in advance, one for each player. You can include things that are there anyway, such as a particular volume in a bookcase or a picture on a wall, or objects that have been specially hidden for the game, like a CD in a laundry basket. Make it as hard or easy as you want.

How to play
One person can plant the items while the others are doing something else. Then it's just a case of turning the hunters loose! Impose a time limit if you don't want the hunt to go on indefinitely.

Change it around ...

If you want to be really smart about it, you can make one found object lead on to the next by leaving a cryptic clue along with it. That way you get to play detective as well as hunter!

Pass the Balloon/Orange

What is it?

If you're looking to break the ice, here's a quick way for your guests to get to know one another better! All they have to do is pass an object between them. If you drop it you're out.

Here's what you need

The only prop required is an item that can be passed from one player to another. Where the fun comes in is in choosing the item and deciding exactly how it's got to be passed.

How to play

With young kids, you might choose a balloon and specify that it has to be passed from one player to another without using the hands and without letting it touch the floor. Or they might use a tennis ball, and only be allowed to move it with their feet.

Teenagers and adults might like to spice things up a bit by using an orange, with the rule being that you have to hold it between your chin and neck – no hands allowed!

Once you've played a round of this, there'll be no going back to trying to look cool or standoffish!

Scissors Open or Closed

What is it?

This is a game in reverse; the game is to learn the rules. Those in the know look serenely enlightened, everyone else looks a fool!

How to play

Get people to sit in a circle. Nominate one person who knows the game to sit apart as the judge. Play starts with the first player passing the scissors to the player on the left, while at the same time saying either 'I pass the scissors open' or 'I pass the scissors closed'. The receiving player replies either 'I receive the scissors open' or 'I receive the scissors closed' before passing them on in turn, saying how they are passing them.

As soon as each exchange is made, the judge has to say whether it is right or wrong. Here's the point: what the players say has nothing to do with whether the *scissors* are actually open or closed! It's the *player* who is 'open' or 'closed' depending on whether their feet (or legs) are uncrossed or crossed!

It's so obvious when you're in the know, but first-timers (unless they're very smart) will be bamboozled!

Truth or Dare?

What is it?

A game of forfeits, where you either have to answer a question truthfully or carry out a dare. There aren't any winners or losers: it's just a way of having fun.

How to play

Decide whose turn it is by spinning a bottle, dealing cards, rolling dice and so on. The real point is what the selected player is asked to do.

When it's your turn you'll be asked if you want Truth or Dare. If you choose Truth, you have to answer a question truthfully, even if it is something you'd rather not discuss! Choose Dare, and you will be dared to do something that would embarrass David Brent.

Some people make it a rule that you can refuse to answer a particular question, but then you *must* take a dare. You can match the nature of the questions and dares to the age level (or level of friskiness!) of those taking part. Be as adult or as childish as you like.

Coin Shuffle

What is it?

A fairly silly game, involving skills that nobody will have had the chance to develop in advance!

Here's what you need

A good supply of coins and a container of some sort for each player. If you don't want your floor or carpet to get wet you might want to put down some sort of protective covering.

How to play

The idea is for players to take a number of coins (as many as they think they can hold!) and grip them between their knees. Then, without using their hands, they have to make their way – which is where the 'shuffle' comes in! – over to a container and position themselves above it so as to drop as many coins as they can into it.

To make it even more difficult, the container should be quite narrow – a mug or beaker would be good (nothing too breakable, of course). Half-filling it with water will stop coins from bouncing right back out but be prepared for splashes to make things a little messy!

Whoever has most coins in the container at the end is the winner. Whether they get to keep their winnings or not is up to you!

The Minister's Cat

What is it?

Who's the Minister? Why does he have a cat? Who cares! This game is all about having fun with words. You don't need any equipment. You don't need a special space. You can play it anywhere, whether you're sitting round the Christmas dinner table or on a long boring car journey to your Auntie's.

How to play

You start with the sentence 'The Minister's Cat is a ----- cat', and each player has to think of a word to put in front of 'cat'. In the first round each player has to use an adjective that begins with the letter A (for example, 'The Minister's Cat is an *angry* cat'). If any player can't spout out a word beginning with A, then he or she is out.

In the next round you have to use words beginning with letter B, and so on, with any defaulters dropping out until all of the letters of the alphabet have been used up. What you do when you get to letter X is up to you! Some people prefer to skip it altogether, while others will allow the use of words beginning with *ex-*.

You can make it quicker by having the first player come up with an adjective beginning with A, the second a word beginning with B, etc.

It can be turned into a memory game, by making each player repeat the adjectives that people have already used as well as adding a new one of their own ('The Minister's Cat is an *angry, beautiful, clever, dreamy* cat' and so on.). But be warned: this version is not for people feeling dozy after a good Christmas dinner!

Chinese Whispers

What is it?

It's all a misunderstanding! There's no winner in this game – everyone gets a good laugh at how whispered messages can turn into something completely different. Why Chinese? Maybe because when the game was invented not many English speakers would have been able to understand Chinese.

How to play

This works best with a fairly large group of people – the more times the message has to be passed, the more chances there are for misunderstandings.

Everyone lines up – make a circle if you like – then the first player thinks up a short message (or it could be a joke, or a line from a hit song) and whispers it to their neighbour, who in turn whispers it to the next person. This goes on until everyone has been involved.

You're not allowed to ask anyone to repeat what they said – you've got to pass it on as you think you heard it. Where the fun comes in is finding out what the last person was told and seeing how it matches up to what the first person said. The end result often doesn't make any sense at all!

Call my Bluff

What is it?

How good are you at bluffing? This game's about trying to convince others that you're the one giving the true definition of an obscure word.

How to play

Start with a good thick dictionary, one that will include words that most people won't be familiar with. Prepare in advance a list of words that seem promising – you can check before play begins that nobody actually knows what they mean. Take one of them and write down its definition on a slip of paper, then make up two more possible definitions (be creative!), write them down, and put them into a hat. The three players for the first round then each draw out a slip.

They now have to 'sell' the definition they have drawn to the rest of the players, who then have to say, in turn, which definition they believe.

How you score the results is up to you, but a popular way of deciding who's winning is to award a point for a player who guesses correctly and two points for a player who manages to convince anyone that their false definition is actually true.

Crambo

What is it?

In this game you have to guess the word that another player has in mind, asking questions that contain a suggestion of what it might be. Rhyming is all important!

How to play

The first player thinks of a word and tells the other players what it rhymes with. They then take turns at asking questions. Let's say the word is 'hand'.

> 1st player: 'I know a word that rhymes with "grand"'.
>
> 2nd player: 'Is it something you find on a beach?'
>
> 1st player: 'No, it isn't "sand"'.
>
> 3rd player: 'Is it something you would listen to?'
>
> 1st player: 'No, it isn't a "band"'.
>
> 4th player: 'Is it something on the end of your arm?'
>
> 1st player: 'Yes, it's a "hand"'.

If someone guesses correctly, they then have a turn at setting the puzzle. If no-one gets it, the first player can have another go.

I Went to Market

What is it?

This is a game designed to test your memory. If you've managed to keep a clear head after the Christmas dinner you'll be in with a shout!

How to play

Play begins with the first player saying what they bought at the market. The second player then has to repeat this and add what they bought too, and so on until the shopping list gets to a very unwieldy length! You can structure it by working through the alphabet, like this:

> 1st player: 'I went to market and bought an **a**ubergine.'

> 2nd player: 'I went to market and bought an aubergine and a **b**iscuit.'

> 3rd player: 'I went to market and bought an aubergine, a biscuit and a **c**andle.'

… and so on. Of course, if you allow choices to be made at random it makes it that much harder to remember when you don't have the alphabet to give you a clue.

To change things around, you could make it that you

84

have to choose from given categories of purchases, like items of clothing, children's toys or kitchen implements … the possibilities are endless. It's your game!

Prop Games

The Maltesers™ Game

What is it?

Never mind 'Don't play with your food', in this game you play with your sweets.

Here's what you need

A bowl of Maltesers™ – if you don't have any, use marshmallows or whatever you like, as long as they don't weigh much. A drinking straw and a cup for each player.

How to play

The idea is to pick up individual sweets from the bowl by putting the end of your straw against each one and sucking hard. Then, without dropping any, carry them away and pop them in your cup by releasing the suction at the right moment.

You have to impose a time limit for each player to grab as many sweets as they can – otherwise they'll keep going until they run out of puff! Thirty seconds should be a reasonable amount of time to allow.

When there's none left in the bowl, the one who has managed to get the most safely into his or her cup is the winner. There are no losers, though – let them all eat what they've got!

Kim's Game

What is it?

This is all about taking note of what you see and committing it to memory. Ideal for young kids and old.

Here's what you need

A tray on which a range of small everyday items are laid out. A cloth to cover this. Paper and a pencil for each player.

How to play

Place a number of ordinary household objects on the tray. A fork, a banana, a mobile phone, a CD … the choice is up to you. Cover everything with a cloth then gather everyone round. Tell them to look carefully and remember what they see. Remove the cloth and leave the objects in view for a minute then cover them up and put the tray away out of sight.

Tell everyone to write down on their paper a list of everything that was on the tray. Award a point for each object correctly remembered (and deduct one for things remembered that weren't actually there!). The winner is the one who scores the most points.

Why the name?

The game is famously described as part of the hero's training as a spy in Rudyard Kipling's novel *Kim* (1901).

Pin the Tail on the Donkey

What is it?

A game for children, exactly what it says on the tin! It will bring a smile to the mouth of even the most intransigent of Eeyores.

Here's what you need

A blindfold is essential. Get someone with artistic leanings to draw a large picture of a donkey on paper, then fix this to a wall. Draw and cut out a number of donkey tails (one each for everyone who wants to play). These will have to be fixed to the big picture, so you'll need drawing pins – or use a solid peelable adhesive if you want to avoid too many holes in the wall.

How to play

Players have to pin their donkey tail where they think it should go, but they have to do it blindfold! Put the blindfold on the first player, then turn them round a couple of times to disorientate them slightly, then give them a little shove in the right general direction. They'll be able to judge from the laughter how off-course they are!

Everyone has a chance, and the winner is the one who gets closest to the right spot.

Balloon Volleyball

What is it?

This kind of volleyball is safe to play indoors, because the 'ball' is a balloon.

Here's what you need

A good-sized, fully-inflated balloon and a length of string or wool to use as a 'net'.

How to play

Tie the ends of the string or wool so that its cuts across a room. Judge the height according to the size of the players. Choose two opposing teams. Just like in volleyball, the idea is to keep passing the balloon from one side of the 'net' to the other.

The team who receives the balloon on their side of the net have to send it back across, without letting it touch the ground, in no more than three 'hits'. If it touches the floor, or they take more than three hits to send it back the other team scores one point.

You can set a target number of points for a win, or just let play go on as long as you like.

Spin the Bottle

What is it?

A kissing game popular with teenagers (and adults too!)

Here's what you need

Any ordinary empty drinks bottle, and a floor surface on which it can spin easily.

How to play

Everyone sits on the floor in a circle, with the bottle in the centre. The first player gives the bottle a spin. When it stops spinning, the first player has to kiss the person that it is judged to be pointing towards. The person who's been kissed then takes a turn at spinning the bottle, and so on.

If you're smart, and watch how the bottle tends to end up, when it's your turn to spin you might just be able to make the bottle point exactly where you want it to go!

Parachute Games

What is it?

These games are based on everyone holding the edges of a parachute.

Here's what you need

Plenty of space and, unsurprisingly enough, a parachute! It doesn't have to be a real one, of course. Toy shops sell specially-designed ones, or you could even make one yourself, if you're handy with a needle and have enough material.

How to play

There's lots of different games you can play, but here's two that all kids will enjoy.

All Change

Get everyone spaced out evenly round the parachute, gripping the edge. Move your arms up and down in unison and the chute will soon get into a rhythm of billowing up and floating gently back down.

As the chute rises, someone calls out a month, and anyone born in that month has to let go and run to the other side before it comes down again.

Sharks

This time everyone sits down with their legs under the chute, still holding on to its edge. They make it act like the waves of the sea by flapping as before, but of course it can't go very high. One person is chosen to be the shark and they crawl about underneath the chute until they select a victim by grabbing their legs. This person then has the chance to stage a realistically gruesome 'death', before taking over as the shark. It's really just an excuse for lots of screaming and overacting!

Hairdryer Pingpong

What is it?

Improvised from everyday objects, this will involve a skill you didn't know you had!

Here's what you need

A hairdryer, some pingpong balls and a container.

How to play

To start, you need to master the art of balancing a pingpong ball in the stream of air coming from a hairdryer. It's not that hard! Keep the dryer at a cold setting so that nobody gets overheated.

Use this method to transport the balls into a container. Obviously, the distance will depend on the length of the flex on the dryer. Introduce obstacles, like a hoop (or a wire coathanger) that you have to pilot your ball through.

The winner is the one who gets most balls into the container.

Games with Music

Name the Tune

What is it?
Players have to identify a piece of music from the opening few bars only.

Here's what you need
A source of music. You can be traditional and have someone playing a piano (if you're lucky enough to have a musician in the company!), or just use any kind of audio player, like an iPod or CD player, as long as you can pause it.

How to play
It's easy! Just listen to the beginning of the piece of music, and as soon as you know what it is, call out the name. You can play as individuals, but competing in teams is usually more fun. The first one to get it right gains one point.

Change it around ...
Since it's the festive season, why not base the game on Christmas Carols? There must be a CD of favourite carols lurking around!

Musical Statues

What is it?

Shake, shake it, shake it, shake, shake it, shake it, STOP!
Shake, shake it…

Here's what you need

Any source of music that can be paused suddenly.

How to play

Press play on your music source (or if you've got a piano
player, give them a nudge!). Any kind of music will do as
long as it's danceable. Everybody dances, or just leaps
about the place, until the music stops. Then they have to
freeze and keep as still as a statue (you can allow heavy
breathing if people are out of puff!) until the music starts
up again.

Last one to freeze is out – and you can also put out
anyone who moves before the music restarts. Spectators
can join in by trying to make the 'statues' move by
making faces at them, telling funny jokes, etc.

Musical Chairs

What's it about?

It's about players moving round a number of chairs while music is being played, then having to suddenly sit down when the music stops without warning. The fun bit is that there's one less chair than there are players, so the one who doesn't get a seat is out. You keep taking away a chair each time until there's only one chair and two players left to fight over it.

Here's what you need

Some empty space and a few ordinary chairs, arranged in a circle or in two rows, back to back. Any room will do, as long as there's plenty of floor space, so clear away the streamers and used crackers. You don't want people tripping up as they zoom round in deadly competition!

Here's where the music comes in

You've got to keep moving while the music's playing (no sneaky holding onto a chair in anticipation!), so why not make it something lively? If you've got a piano, get someone to bash out a stomping rhythm. Otherwise use anything recorded, as long as there's 'play' and 'pause' buttons.

Pass the Parcel

What is it?

This is ideal for Christmas parties with lots of young kids. They all get turns to tear off a level of wrapping on the way to a surprise present!

Here's what you need

Get together some small Christmas gifts that are suitable for both boys and girls. You'll need plenty of wrapping paper – why not recycle some that's been used already, as long as it's not too torn up? Wrap each present in lots of different-coloured layers of paper.

How to play

The kids sit in a circle and pass the parcel from one to another while music is played. When the music suddenly stops, the person holding the parcel tears off one layer of wrapping paper. The music then restarts and the parcel starts moving until the music stops again. It's amazing how reluctant people become to let go of the parcel! Carry on doing this until one person gets to remove the last layer and – congratulations! – the present is theirs to keep!

To avoid tears and envious pouting, the person in charge of the music can cleverly time things to make sure no-one finishes the game empty-handed!

Guessing Games

Animal, Vegetable, Mineral

What is it?

In this guessing game you have to work out what someone has in mind by asking them questions.

How to play

The first player decides what they want the others to guess but doesn't tell anyone. The others then take turns in asking them a question, to which the answer must be simply 'yes' or 'no' (no lying allowed!). Some people limit the number of possible questions to twenty (which gives the game its other popular name, 'Twenty Questions'), but rules like that are up to you.

A good way to get things going is to make the first question 'Are you animal, vegetable or mineral?' That shrinks the field quite nicely! Questions can't be complicated – otherwise they can't be answered with a yes or no – and the trick is to make sure each question narrows down the possibilities as much as possible.

Size is a good approach: you could ask, for example, 'Is it bigger than a football?' 'Can you eat it?' is another genre-defining line of attack. If you think you've worked it out, you can ask the direct question, such as

'Is it a dolphin?'

The winner is the one who guesses correctly. If nobody gets it, the first player has another go.

What's my Line?

What is it?

This game is all about guessing what someone does for a living by asking them simple questions.

How to play

The player who's 'it' chooses an occupation (it doesn't have to be their own real one!) without letting anyone else know. The others then take turns asking questions which must be straightforward enough to be answered 'yes' or 'no'.

The skill lies in moving the questions on from being very general (like, 'Do you make a product?' or 'Do you work with other people?') to the more specific (like 'Do you use a computer?'). Keep the questions coming until someone feels that they can make a reasonable guess, like 'Are you a taxi driver?'

You can make a guess at any point. The player who guesses correctly wins and then it's their turn.

Botticelli

What is it?

Here's where you get to show off your knowledge about famous people by guessing the right one.

How to play

The first player (the chooser) secretly picks a famous person, says what letter the name (usually the surname, unless the person is famous enough to have only one, like Madonna) begins with, and invites the other players to work out who it is by asking questions.

We've all got different ideas about who is and isn't famous, of course – somebody you think *everybody* will know of can turn out to be the next person's idea of total obscurity! So, the rule of thumb is that any person chosen must be at least as famous as the artist Botticelli (So *that's* why they call it that!). That way all the players have a good chance of being able to ask and answer reasonable questions.

The questioners' task is to narrow down the possibilities by posing questions that the chooser has to answer 'yes' or 'no'. For example, let's say the chosen person is Davina McCall, so the chooser says the relevant letter is 'M'.

A questioner might ask 'Are you a musician?' The chooser then tries to guess who the questioner is thinking of and might reply 'No, I am not Paul McCartney'. If this is who the questioner was thinking of, then the next questioner gets a turn; if it's not, then the questioner can pose another question. If the chooser has no idea who the questioner means, then he or she has to say 'Yes, but I don't know who you're thinking of' and the questioner gets another turn.

Play goes on like this until someone works it out. Be warned, though, this can take rather a long time!

What is it?

What is What is it?

In this game players have to work out what various objects are simply by touch – because they're blindfolded!

Here's what you need

Just a range of everyday objects that are to be found around the house. If kids are playing, nothing too big or heavy for small hands to cope with, and, of course, nothing with sharp edges. And a blindfold!

How to play

Decide who is going first and send them out of the room. You can place the objects on a table and have the guesser feel his or her way along them, or you might prefer to have them sit down and have the objects placed in their hands.

Players score a point for every item they identify correctly, but half the fun is hearing them get something completely wrong or fail to work out what it is at all!

It's up to you whether or not you want to play tactile tricks on the blindfolded victim. Having your fingers plunged into a bowl of jam, cold Christmas pudding or a soft-boiled egg can be an unpleasant surprise when you can't see what it is, especially if other people are giggling like mad or retching.

I Spy

What is it?

Can you work out what it is that someone else has their eye on?

Here's what you need

Very little! Just the ability to keep your eyes open … and, of course, it helps if you can spell! You can play it anywhere and get started with no preparation at all.

How to play

The first player decides on something that he or she can see that the others will have to guess, and says 'I spy, with my little eye, something beginning with … (here you say the relevant letter of the alphabet)'. It can be anything as long as it's as easy for the others to see as it is for you. Don't let them catch you gazing directly at it though! Try to be looking at something else when you make your announcement, just to throw them off the track.

The others now look around and call out the names of any object they see that begins with the nominated letter. Set a time limit, say five minutes, otherwise the game could go on and on. The first person to guess correctly wins the right to choose the next object.

Who Am I?

What is it?

This game's for people who don't know who they are while their identity is clear to everyone else!

How to play

Someone writes the names of lots of famous people on individual yellow sticky notes and puts them into a hat or other non-see-through container. Each player then pulls a note out of the hat and, without, reading it, sticks it on their forehead so that they can't see what it says.

Each player tries to work out who they're meant to be, by taking a turn to ask the group a question. The others are only allowed to answer 'yes' or 'no', and if the questioner gets a 'yes' he or she can then ask another question.
Or they can make a guess at their identity at any time.
Once they get a 'no' answer the turn to ask questions passes to the next player.

Warning: this game can lead to extreme hilarity! Because everybody else knows the right answer, the questioner's puzzlement and silly guesses provide no end of fun.

Psychiatrist

What is it?

You don't have to be crazy to play this game … but it helps! It's all about correctly identifying the particular kind of psychiatric problem that people claim to be suffering from.

How to play

There are no props required. Just get everybody sitting in a circle. Choose who goes first then send that person out of the room. While they're away, everyone else agrees on a 'psychiatric illness' that they're all going to be victims of.

This can be whatever you like, from phobias, like a fear of spiders, to delusions, like believing you are Napoleon Bonaparte or Kate Winslet. The more you use your imaginations, the harder it'll be for the nominated player to work it out!

Bring the first player back into the room and sit them in the middle. They are now the 'psychiatrist' and everyone else is a 'patient'. The psychiatrist tries to identify the affliction they all share by asking individuals questions, like 'Are you afraid of something?' or 'What do you like to do best?'

The patient questioned must reply, but the trick is to give as little away as possible in your answer, thus keeping the psychiatrist guessing! If a patient gives an answer that is untrue or isn't really consistent with what they're supposed to be suffering from, then one of the other patients can shout 'Psychiatrist!' Then the two patients have to exchange seats, so the psychiatrist finds it harder to keep track of who said what and who gave the wrong information.

Play ends when the psychiatrist correctly diagnoses the affliction, provided they haven't been driven nuts already!